Unity Creates the Shell... Strength is! Guide to Individual Strength and Conscious Unity for Building a Positive Future

Preface

Welcome to a journey of inner and collective exploration, a path through the power of individual strength and the art of conscious unity. In this book, titled "Unity Creates the Shell... Strength is!" we will delve into profound and transformative concepts aimed at illuminating the path towards a positive future.

The key philosophy guiding this exploration is encapsulated in the saying "Unity Creates the Shell... Strength is!" A perspective that not only challenges the traditional concept of strength derived from unity but reveals a deeper truth: strength already resides within us. Unity, when guided by positive principles, becomes the "shell" that protects and preserves the future of positive creation.

These pages invite you to explore the strength within you, to make enlightened choices that not only shape your personal destiny but also contribute to the common good. Each chapter is a piece of knowledge, an opportunity for reflection and growth.

From recognizing individual strength to constructive criticism of the popular saying "Unity is strength," from delving into the concept of strength as a conscious choice to awareness of the dangers of negative aggregation, this book offers a journey rich in insights for personal and collective transformation.

Through the beauty of positive unity, the analysis of mental mafia and destructive emotions, and the defense of individual strength against negative aggregations, we will explore how each individual can contribute to creating a more positive society.

The transformation of negative energy according to the Argentine philosophy, the creation of the "shell" that protects the future, and strategies to defend against attacks from negative aggregations are fundamental steps in the proposed journey.

We conclude our journey with an invitation to recognize that strength is a journey, not a destination. Every choice, every action contributes to the tapestry of our personal and collective story. Strength is within you, ready to guide you towards a positive future.

Take this book not only as a guide but as a companion on your journey. May each page be a source of inspiration, a call to action, and a reminder that strength is an intrinsic gift that, when cultivated with awareness, illuminates the path towards a future of growth, prosperity, and common good.

Safe travels!

Chapter 1: Introduction - The Art of Individual Strength

In the vast theater of life, each individual is called to play their role with a unique and unrepeated strength. The essence of this strength lies in self-awareness and the ability to make enlightened choices, thus transforming one's existence into a continuously evolving work of art.

Strength as Individual Expression:

In a world often characterized by hustle and external pressures, it is crucial to recognize the intrinsic potential residing in each individual. Individual strength is not merely a characteristic but rather an opportunity to express oneself in a unique and authentic way. It is the art of shaping one's own destiny through thoughtful choices, resolute actions, and positive outcomes.

Developing Strength Through Conscious Choices:

Individual strength thrives on conscious choices. Every decision, whether big or small, is a brushstroke painting the canvas of our existence. By acknowledging the power of our choices, we can shape our path in ways that reflect our authenticity and guide us towards deeper fulfillment.

The Art of Resolute Actions:

Actions are the means through which individual strength finds tangible expression in the world. Facing challenges with determination, pursuing goals with passion, and acting resolutely are the brushes that create the distinctive strokes of our personal masterpiece. Each positive action contributes to a crescendo of strength permeating our lives.

Positive Outcomes: The Manifestation of Strength:

Individual strength reaches its pinnacle in the positive outcomes we generate. Achieving goals, creating meaningful impacts, and building healthy relationships are tangible testimonies of the strength flowing through us. These outcomes not only enrich our lives but also illuminate the path for others.

Invitation to the Art of Individual Strength:

This book is an invitation to embark on a journey of personal discovery, to recognize one's strength as a continuously evolving art form. Through the exploration of concepts, stories, and practical examples, we will delve into the depths of individual awareness, opening the doors to

the creation of a unique
masterpiece.

Let's unveil the secrets of the art
of individual strength, for every
page of this book will be a blank
canvas on which to paint our
unique and unrepeatable path in
the quest for inner strength.

Chapter 2: The Deception of the Popular Saying: "Unity Creates Strength"

In the extensive repertoire of popular sayings that have shaped our perception of reality, few are as deeply ingrained in our culture as the ancient adage "Unity Creates Strength." However, behind its apparent wisdom lies a deception that can lead to detrimental outcomes when unity lacks positive and noble principles.

The Traditional Vision: A Noble and Constructive Union:

Let us begin by acknowledging the positive side of this popular saying. The idea of joining forces to face common challenges, build communities, and work together for the common good is inherently valid. However, like any double-edged sword, the strength of unity can be distorted when not guided by positive principles.

The Deception of Negative Aggregation: Mental Mafia and Destructive Emotions:

Unity is not automatically synonymous with positive strength. In many contexts, negative aggregation can manifest as "mental mafia," where groups of individuals come together not to pursue noble goals but to fuel destructive emotions such as envy, anger, and jealousy. In this way, unity becomes a weapon against those who stand out for their intelligence or success, creating a negative spiral of harmful behaviors.

The Risk of Conformity: Surrendering Individuality:

Another insidious trap of unity not guided by positive principles is conformity. When individuals come together without maintaining their individuality and autonomy of thought, the result can be the loss of the uniqueness that defines them. This phenomenon can lead to a kind of "groupthink" that suppresses creativity and innovation.

Lesson from the Evil Union: When Unity is Destructive:

Let's closely examine historical and contemporary examples where unity has been used as a tool for destruction. From thought control cults to criminal organizations, such cases demonstrate how unity without positive principles can become a dark force, capable of undermining stability and well-being.

The New Interpretation: Guiding Unity with Noble Principles:

We must rewrite the popular saying to adapt it to a more comprehensive and positive view: "Unity Creates the Shell... Strength is!" This suggests that strength is already present in every individual, and unity can become a protective shell when guided by noble principles. Unity must be a weapon for good, not for evil.

Reflection Guide: Individual Strength as a Prerequisite to Unity:

We conclude the chapter by inviting readers to reflect on their individual strength before seeking unity with others. Only individuals aware of their own strength can contribute to a positive and constructive unity. Individual strength must precede and guide unity, creating a solid foundation for the creation of a better world.

In this chapter, we have looked beyond the surface of the popular saying, revealing the dark nuances of unity not guided by noble principles. True strength resides not only in unity but in the awareness and guidance of positive principles that can transform aggregation into a constructive and beneficial force for all.

Chapter 3: The Force as Conscious Choice: The Power of Awareness

The true force, one that permeates every aspect of our existence, resides in the illumination of awareness. In this chapter, we will explore how self-awareness is the foundation upon which individual strength stands, transforming daily choices into a work of art that carves the path of our lives.

Awareness as the Key to Understanding Existence:

Imagine awareness as a penetrating light that dispels the shadows of ignorance. It allows us to look within, to understand our thoughts, emotions, and actions with a clarity that goes beyond the surface. Awareness is the key to understanding existence, a beacon that illuminates every corner of our being.

Recognizing One's Inner Strength:

Self-awareness is the first step in recognizing the strength within each of us. It is the ability to observe without judgment, to accept our weaknesses and, at the same time, acknowledge our latent potentials. When we become aware of our inner strength, we can begin to shape our destiny with enlightened choices.

Choosing with Intention: The Art of Enlightened Choices:

Strength is not merely a static characteristic; it is dynamic, manifesting through the choices we make every day. Enlightened choices are those made with intention and awareness. Instead of acting impulsively or reactively, we approach decisions with thoughtful attention, considering the consequences and impact on our lives and those of others.

The Strength of Resilience: Embracing and Growing:

Awareness endows us with the ability to face challenges with resilience. When we fully understand our capabilities and limitations, we can accept adversity without succumbing. Resilience is a tangible manifestation of inner strength, enabling us to transform life's trials into opportunities for growth.

Authenticity as a Manifestation of Strength:

Awareness also guides us toward authenticity. Being true to ourselves requires a deep awareness of our beliefs, values, and aspirations. When we live in harmony with our authenticity, we become an irresistible force that positively influences others and the world around us.

Practicing Mindfulness: Training Inner Strength:

Awareness can be cultivated through the practice of mindfulness. It teaches us to live in the present moment, to be aware of our experiences without being overwhelmed by the past or anxious about the future. Mindfulness is a training for inner strength, helping us maintain calm, clarity, and wisdom in the most complex situations.

Conclusion: Illuminating the Path of Strength:

In conclusion, individual strength finds its roots in self-awareness. This chapter is an invitation to explore the power of awareness, to recognize the inner strength that already resides in each of us. Only through enlightened choices,

made with intention and
awareness, can we transform our
lives into an ever-evolving
masterpiece, fueled by the
brilliant light of our inner strength.

Chapter 4: The Danger of Negative Aggregation: Mental Mafia and Destructive Emotions

As we delve into the analysis of negative aggregation, we enter a complex and often dark territory where connections between individuals can transform into a destructive force. In this chapter, we will closely examine how negative aggregation, fueled by destructive emotions, can give rise to harmful behaviors, leading to the formation of what we can define as a "mental mafia."

Formation of the Mental Mafia: A Dark Pact:

Negative aggregation begins with individuals sharing negative emotions such as envy, anger, or resentment. These emotions become the glue that binds the group together, forming a "mental mafia." In this dark pact, individuals converge to pursue a common goal: to harm, suppress, or destroy someone or something they perceive as a threat.

Destructive Emotions as Fuel:

Destructive emotions, like envy and anger, act as fuel for negative aggregation. Envy can morph into a sick desire to diminish others, while anger becomes a catalyst for vindictive actions. These emotions, when collectively cultivated, fuel the "mental mafia" machine, making it increasingly powerful in pursuing its destructive goals.

The Vicious Cycle of Collective Mind:

Negative aggregation creates a vicious cycle within the "mental mafia." Individuals share and reinforce their destructive

emotions through constant
communication and interaction.
The group becomes fertile ground
for cultivating malevolent ideas
and plans, further fueling the
destructive cycle.

**Resonance of Negative
Emotions:**

Negative aggregation creates a
resonance of negative emotions
within the group. Emotions
intensify through mutual
feedback, transforming into a
disruptive force that guides the
collective's actions. The collective
mind feeds on these emotions,
pushing the group towards
increasingly harmful behaviors.

The Role of Group Identity:

Group identity within the "mental
mafia" becomes a key
component. Individuals
strengthen their belonging to the
group, increasingly identifying
with the common goal. This group

identity can overshadow individuality, leading to collective blindness to the moral consequences of their actions.

Consequences of Negative Aggregation: Destruction and Suffering:

Negative aggregation, when evolving into a "mental mafia," inevitably leads to destructive consequences. The group's common goal can manifest through harmful actions towards individuals, organizations, or ideas deemed hostile. These actions can cause suffering, destroy reputations, and jeopardize social stability.

Defense Strategies: Breaking the Cycle of Negative Aggregation:

We conclude by exploring defense strategies against negative aggregation. These strategies include promoting individual awareness of emotions, educating on the management of destructive emotions, and building communities based on positive values. Breaking the cycle of negative aggregation requires a collective commitment to promote awareness and build a culture of mutual respect.

In this chapter, we have plumbed the depths of the danger associated with negative aggregation, highlighting how destructive emotions and group identity can converge into harmful behaviors. Understanding this complex dynamic is crucial for developing effective defenses and promoting a society based on positive cooperation rather than mutual destruction.

Chapter 5: The Beauty of Positive Union: Noble Choices and Common Goals

In a world often characterized by tensions and conflicts, the positive aspect of aggregation emerges when guided by noble values and common goals. In this chapter, we will explore the beauty of positive union, examining how enlightened choices and altruistic intentions can shape a future based on cooperation, contributing to the common good.

Guidance of Noble Values:

Positive union begins with the guidance of noble values. When individuals come together with respect, integrity, and empathy as foundations, aggregation becomes a vehicle for progress and growth. The beauty of union lies in building relationships based on mutual trust and the sharing of ethical principles.

Enlightened Choices: An Evolving Art:

Positive union manifests through enlightened choices, where each decision is imbued with awareness and responsibility. Enlightened choices reflect the beauty of individuals who, while maintaining their individuality, collaborate for the common good. Each choice becomes an evolving work of art, shaped by an awareness of its impact on the community and the world.

Harmony of Common Goals:

The beauty of positive union expands when individuals converge towards common goals. These goals are not selfish or limited to individual pursuits but aim for collective improvement. The harmony of common goals

creates a symphony of
coordinated actions contributing
to the common good, elevating
the quality of life for all.

**The Beauty of Altruistic
Contribution:**

Positive union finds its fullest
expression in altruistic
contribution. When individuals
unite to serve others without
expecting anything in return, a
profound and meaningful beauty
unfolds. This altruistic spirit
creates a social fabric where
kindness, solidarity, and
compassion become guiding
stars.

**Collective Benefit: A Message
of Hope:**

Positive union creates a virtuous
circle of collective benefits. When
individuals come together to
pursue positive goals, the results
reflect a tangible improvement in
the quality of life for everyone.

This is a message of hope indicating the possibility of building a future where aggregation is synonymous with progress and well-being.

The Strength of Diversity in Positive Union:

Explore how diversity, when positively embraced, becomes a strength in union. The beauty of positive aggregation fully manifests when individuals with diverse perspectives unite, bringing a richness of ideas, cultures, and skills. This diversity becomes the lifeblood that fuels innovation and evolution.

Challenges and Strategies for Lasting Positive Union:

Address the challenges that may arise even in positive union and propose strategies to overcome them. Awareness of potential challenges, such as conflict management and preserving individuality, is crucial to ensure a lasting and meaningful positive union.

Conclusion: The Beauty of a United World for the Common Good:

Conclude this chapter by opening a window to the beauty of a world where union is guided by noble choices and common goals. The beauty lies in the art of creating a future where positive aggregation is a beacon of hope, an opportunity to build a better world for present and future generations.

Through the exploration of the beauty of positive union, we draw closer to a framework of coexistence based on cooperation, love, and altruism, where the strength of aggregation becomes a force for the common good.

Chapter 6: Defending Individual Strength: Resisting Negative Aggregation

In the journey of life, individuals often face challenges stemming from negative aggregations. In this chapter, we will explore strategies for defending individual strength, providing individuals with the tools needed to resist the attacks of negative aggregations and transform negative energy into positive force.

Understanding the Dynamics of Negative Aggregation:

The first step in defending individual strength is understanding the dynamics of negative aggregation. We will analyze how ill-intentioned individuals come together to pursue harmful goals and how these aggregations can negatively influence the lives of positive individuals. Awareness is the foundation upon which to build an effective defense.

Fortifying Inner Strength:

Defending individual strength begins with fortifying inner strength. Good individuals must cultivate a deep awareness of their skills, values, and goals. This process of self-discovery provides a solid foundation on which to resist external negative influences, maintaining one's identity and integrity.

Developing a Resilient Mindset:

Resilience is one of the most powerful weapons in defense against negative aggregation. We will explore how to develop a resilient mindset that enables individuals to face challenges without succumbing. Resilience helps transform difficulties into opportunities for growth, keeping individual strength intact even in the most challenging times.

Managing Negative Emotions: Transforming Energy:

Negative emotions can be like arrows launched by negative aggregations. We will examine strategies for managing these emotions in a healthy and transformative way. Transforming negative energy into positive is an act of resistance and self-defense that allows good individuals to maintain mental clarity and fortitude.

Learning to Say No: Enforcing Healthy Boundaries:

Defending individual strength requires the ability to say no when necessary. We will explore the art of enforcing healthy boundaries, recognizing when participation in an aggregation might be harmful. Imposing clear limits is essential for preserving one's integrity and protecting individual strength.

Seeking Positive Support: Building Healthy Alliances:

Individual strength finds support in positive aggregation. We will examine how seeking the support of positive individuals and building healthy alliances can fortify resistance against negative aggregations. Uniting with people who share similar values creates a protective shield against harmful influences.

Educating Oneself on Manipulative Tactics: Being Vigilant and Prepared:

Effective defense requires knowledge of manipulative tactics used by negative aggregations. Good individuals must be vigilant and prepared, educating themselves on manipulative strategies that might be employed. Awareness is the first line of defense against attacks seeking to undermine individual strength.

Cultivating Compassion as a Shield:

Compassion is a powerful shield against the aggression of negative aggregations. We will explore how cultivating compassion for oneself and others can neutralize negative energy, transforming it into a force for connection and healing. Compassion is a force that elevates individual strength, rendering it immune to negative intentions.

Conclusion: A Vigilant Defense for Individual Strength:

In conclusion, defending individual strength is an ongoing and conscious process. Good individuals must be vigilant, prepared, and committed to cultivating strength that is shielded from harmful influences.

This chapter offers an arsenal of
strategies to resist negative
aggregation and transform
challenges into opportunities for
growth and affirmation of
individual strength.

Chapter 7: Transforming Negative Energy: "Algo malo, in algo bueno"

In Argentine culture, there is a powerful and wisdom-infused philosophy that states "Algo malo, in algo bueno," translating to "Something bad, into something good." In this chapter, we will delve deeply into this philosophy and how the transformation of negative energy can lead to long-term victories. We will discover strategies to adopt this approach in everyday life.

Understanding the Essence of "Algo malo, in algo bueno":

The core of this philosophy lies in the ability to transform negative experiences into opportunities for growth and positive change. We begin with a detailed examination of how the Argentine perspective can inform our daily actions, urging us to see beyond initial adversities.

The Strength of an Optimistic Perspective:

An optimistic perspective is a crucial starting point in transforming negative energy. We examine how to develop an attitude that, even in the face of challenges, sees the potential for something positive. This does not mean denying reality but rather adopting a filter that allows us to extract positive teachings from difficult situations.

Creativity in Facing Adversities:

We explore how creativity can be a precious resource in transforming negative energy. A creative approach enables us to find innovative solutions to problems, turning obstacles into opportunities. Creativity thus becomes a powerful ally in the transformation process.

Resilience as the Foundation of Transformation:

Resilience is a key element in facing negative energy and transforming it into something positive. We analyze how developing resilience is essential to overcome adversities and how this attitude can lead to long-term victories. Resilience is the flexibility that allows us to bend but not break in the face of difficulties.

The Power of Reflection:

The Argentine philosophy suggests that reflecting on negative experiences is a fundamental step in energy transformation. We explore how deep reflection on challenging circumstances can help us better understand ourselves, appreciate the lessons learned, and benefit from the challenges.

Long-Term Vision:

One of the most powerful features of "Algo malo, in algo bueno" is its connection to a long-term vision. We analyze how this perspective can guide our daily actions, urging us not to focus solely on immediate defeat but rather on the long-term victory that can emerge from the transformation of negative energy.

Concrete Strategies for Transformation:

We offer concrete strategies to implement the Argentine philosophy in everyday life. These strategies include mindfulness practices, stress management techniques, and adopting a proactive approach in seeking growth opportunities even in the most challenging situations.

Success Stories: Inspirational Transformations:

We conclude the chapter with success stories that illustrate how individuals have transformed seemingly negative situations into positive outcomes. These stories serve as inspiration, demonstrating the transformative potential of the philosophy "Algo malo, in algo bueno." Through a profound exploration of the Argentine philosophy, we learn that transforming negative energy requires an open perspective, creativity, resilience, and a long-term vision. This approach not only helps us overcome adversities but also guides us toward lasting victories that arise from the act of transforming negative energy into something good.

Chapter 8: Building the Shield: Safeguarding the Future of Positive Creation

We now enter the crucial phase of our exploration, where we will address how individuals aware of their strength can come together to create a protective "shield," thus safeguarding the future of their positive creation. We will examine how this "shield" can act as a bulwark against negative influences and preserve the positive impact of collective actions.

Awareness of Individual Strength:

We begin with the importance of awareness of individual strength. Individuals must recognize and embrace their intrinsic power, understanding how their choices, actions, and outcomes impact not only their lives but also the broader social fabric. This awareness forms the foundation upon which to build the protective "shield."

Conscious Union for Noble Goals:

Conscious aggregation must be guided by noble goals. We explore how individuals aware of their strength can deliberately unite, selecting aggregation partners carefully and sharing a common vision. This conscious union is the first layer of the "shield" that will protect positive creation.

Sharing Ethical Principles:

The protective "shield" is reinforced by the sharing of solid ethical principles. Individuals must commit to following values such as integrity, kindness, and responsibility. These principles become the cement that holds the "shield" together and ensures its resilience to external negative pressures.

Open and Constructive Communication:

We examine the crucial role of open and constructive communication within the protective "shield." Individuals must be able to express ideas, concerns, and goals clearly and respectfully. Effective communication is a key element in building a strong and resilient "shield."

Cultivating Collective Resilience:

Collective resilience is a fundamental element in protecting the future of positive creation. We explore how individuals within the "shield" can support each other in times of difficulty, sharing lessons learned and transforming challenges into opportunities for growth. Collective resilience is the connective tissue that keeps the "shield" intact.

Adaptability to Contextual Complexity:

The creation of the "shield" must be adaptable to the complexity of the surrounding context. Individuals must be able to review and adapt their protection strategies in response to changes and new challenges. Adaptability is a key element to ensure that the "shield" remains effective over time.

Valuing Diversity:

We explore how valuing diversity can contribute to the solidity of the "shield." The diversity of perspectives, skills, and experiences enriches the "shield," making it more resilient and capable of facing a variety of situations. Valuing diversity is an investment in the robustness of protection.

Sustainability Over Time:

The "shield" must be sustainable over time. Individuals aware of their strength must commit to maintaining and strengthening the "shield" over time, ensuring that it continues to protect positive creation in the long run. This requires constant commitment and shared vigilance.

Positive Contribution to Society:

Finally, we explore how the "shield" can not only protect the positive creation of those involved but also positively contribute to the broader society. The "shield" can become a beacon of inspiration, demonstrating how conscious union can lead to lasting results and widespread benefits.

Conclusion: The "Shield" as Custodian of the Common Good:

We conclude this chapter by reflecting on the "shield" as a custodian of the common good. The creation and maintenance of this "shield" require commitment, awareness, and collective actions. When individuals aware of their strength come together to build this "shield," they become the guardians

Chapter 9: Conclusion: The Strength Is Within You

We arrive at the heart of our journey, where we consolidate fundamental concepts and inspire readers to recognize and cultivate the strength that resides within them. In this final phase, we will examine how each individual can make choices that contribute to the common good, thus shaping a positive future.

Summary of Key Concepts:

- **Conscious Individual Strength:** We explored individual strength as a result of positive choices, actions, and outcomes, emphasizing the importance of self-awareness and the ability to make enlightened choices.

- **Debunking the Popular Saying:** We critically examined the saying "Strength in unity," recognizing that aggregation must occur in positive contexts and be guided by noble goals to avoid negative consequences.

- **Strength as a Conscious Choice:** We delved into the concept that true strength lies in self-awareness and the ability to make conscious choices, thus illuminating the path to authentic strength.

- **Danger of Negative Aggregation:** We analyzed how negative aggregation can lead to destructive behaviors, such as mental mobs and negative emotions, emphasizing the need to defend against such influences.

- **Beauty of Positive Union:** We explored how union guided by noble values and common goals can be positive, contributing to the common good and creating a "shield" that protects positive creation.

- **Defense of Individual Strength:** We offered strategies to defend against the attacks of negative aggregations, transforming negative energy into positive and maintaining individual strength intact.

- **Transformation of Negative Energy:** We delved into the Argentine philosophy of transforming negative energy into positive, exploring how this approach can lead to long-term victories.

- **Creation of the Shield:** We discussed how individuals aware of their strength can come together to create a "shield" that protects the future of their positive creation, examining the fundamental principles for its construction.

Encouraging the Discovery of Inner Strength:

The conclusion of this journey is an invitation to every reader to explore the strength within themselves. Strength is not a gift reserved for a few but an intrinsic potential in each of us. We encourage readers to look within, recognize their abilities, make enlightened choices, and pursue positive outcomes.

Making Choices that Contribute to the Common Good:

Individual strength takes on meaning when our actions contribute to the common good. Every choice, big or small, has an impact. We encourage readers to consider how their daily actions can be a positive contribution to the world around them.

Supporting and Inspiring Others:

Individual strength can be contagious. We encourage readers to share their strength with others, support those in need, and be a source of inspiration. In this way, strength spreads, creating a network of positivity that embraces the broader community.

Cultivating Awareness and Resilience:

Self-awareness and resilience are the keys to maintaining and cultivating inner strength. We invite readers to practice mindfulness, face challenges with resilience, and learn from experiences, thus shaping a strength that grows over time.

Strength is a Journey, Not a Destination:

We remind readers that strength is a continuous journey, not a destination. Each day offers new opportunities to develop inner strength and contribute to the common good. We are the authors of our story, and strength is the pen with which we write our path.

An Invitation to Be Agents of Positive Change:

We conclude this chapter and our book with an invitation to be agents of positive change. Every choice, every action can be a step toward a better future. May every reader feel called to explore the strength within themselves and contribute to the common good, thus becoming a bright beacon in the vastness of the universe we all share. Strength is within you, ready to illuminate your path.

Conclusion: Illuminating the Path of Strength

We have reached the end of this journey through individual strength and conscious union. In these pages, we have explored the profound truth that "Union Creates the Shield... Strength Is!" and discovered how each of us possesses the potential to contribute to a positive future.

The Power of Your Inner Strength:

Always remember that strength is an intrinsic gift, a light that resides within you. Every choice, every action can be guided by this inner strength, shaping your personal path.

The Beauty of Positive Union:

We explored how union can be a positive force when guided by noble values. The "shield" created through this union becomes the guardian of the common good, protecting the future of our positive creation.

Defend and Transform:

You have learned to defend against the attacks of negative aggregations, transforming negative energy into an engine of positive change. This transformative ability is one of your greatest strengths.

Call to Action:

Now, the call to action is for you. Reflect on what you have learned and integrate these concepts into your daily life. Be aware of your choices, join those who share noble values, and contribute to the common good.

The journey of strength is a continuous path. Be the architects of your destiny and agents of positive change in society. Every step you take is a contribution to the broader fabric of the common good.

Strength Is Within You:

Finally, always remember that strength is within you. Be an inspiration to others, spread the light of your individual strength, and contribute to creating a future where everyone can thrive.
Thank you for being companions on this journey. May strength always be your beacon, illuminating the path of your life and inspiring others to do the same.
Your journey continues. Strength is within you. Onward with courage!

Federico Carminati

www.ingramcontent.com/pod-product-compliance
Lightning Source LLC
Chambersburg PA
CBHW031331250726
48656CB00005B/2069